# Shocking Spree Killers: True, Horrific, and Puzzling Stories of Cold Blooded Murderers

Disclaimer and Terms of Use: Effort has been made to ensure that the information in this book is accurate and complete, however, the author and the publisher do not warrant the accuracy of the information, text and graphics contained within the book due to the rapidly changing nature of science, research, known and unknown facts and internet. The Author and the publisher do not hold any responsibility for errors, omissions or contrary interpretation of the subject matter herein. This book is presented solely for motivational and informational purposes only.

# Table of Contents

# Introduction

Murder.  The definition of murder, or homicide, is the act of taking another person's life.  In the United States of America, murder has several sub-classifications including, but not limited to, the following: murder in the first, murder in the second, involuntary manslaughter, voluntary manslaughter, and many more.  Murder in the first degree occurs when the murder is pre-meditated and the intent of the person is to ensure the victim is dead.  There is only a slight difference between murder in the first degree and murder in the second degree.  The difference between the two lies in the intent of the person.  If the intent was to cause significant bodily injury but not death, then that is when the crime becomes murder in the second degree.

Third degree murder often is considered as 'manslaughter' by the court system.  Again, the primary focus is intent of the accused.  Voluntary manslaughter is something that many people know as 'passion killings' which there was no premeditation involved whereas involuntary manslaughter happens when an individual's recklessness causes another person's death such as the case with drunk drivers.

Yet, there is no specific classification for some of the vilest acts in society above murder in the first degree.  These acts are spree killings.  Spree killers pick off their victims at random most of the time, but do so in large numbers all at once or over a very short time period.  They do this for nothing more than the thrill of the hunt.  Most spree killers are the same as serial killers with regard to the fact that serial killers do so over years and rarely ever stopped.  Spree killers have slightly more control over themselves.  Anyone can be the target.  Some are like serial killers in the respect that a specific type of victim as was the case with Charles Arthur 'Pretty Boy' Floyd or Richard Speck.  In more recent times, there are some people who are more likely to recall the likes of Anders Behring Brevik.  Regardless of body count, the biggest question often remains: Why?

All murder is horrendous and heart wrenching for the families of those slain, but mankind's hidden darkness is exposed by those who create such terror among the innocents.

# Anders Brevik

On a hot summer day in July 2011, six hundred teenagers aged fourteen to nineteen were attending a summer camp on the island of Utoya. Utoya is an island that is part of Norway and is often a vacation spot for the local teens and some tourists. The teens are enjoying themselves and talking. Meanwhile, a man by the name of Anders Behring Brevik is driving his car toward Oslo. Once he arrives, he parks the car in front of the government building that houses the Prime Minister of Norway and leaves it. As he boards the ferry to the island of Utoya, wearing a police uniform he acquired at a surplus shop, the car bomb made from fertilizer and fuel oil that he placed in the vehicle detonated. Eight people died in the massive explosion, and two hundred and nine more found themselves seriously injured.

The ferry arrives with Brevik to Utoya Island where, clad in police uniform, Brevik gains entrance to the camp with the identification badge he forged and tells the campers to gather around him for the purpose of a security check so that he could get a head count. He told them the reason for this was the bombing that just occurred in Oslo a few moments prior. As the campers gathered around him, Brevik produced a Ruger mini-14 Ranch rifle with a semiautomatic carbine and began spraying bullets into the crowd. Once he ran out of ammunition for the rifle, he resorted to his Glock 34 semiautomatic pistol.

Those who managed to survive the horror of the murders on Utoya Island claimed that Brevik laughed as he committed these acts. He especially found it entertaining when those he murdered begged for their lives. According to some accounts, some people attempted to thwart his attempts on their life by playing dead, but Brevik did not fall for it. He made another round and shot many bodies for a second time. Those who attempted to escape in the water were shot in such a manner as to force them to die by drowning. Only a few managed to escape through the water due to efforts of nearby boaters who came to assist.

Many of those who survived did so by hiding in the underground restrooms and used their cell phones to communicate. Brevik's reign of terror lasted ninety minutes before the real police arrived. Brevik surrendered without incident. Through investigation of the two incidents, after police realized the same man caused the bombing and the massacre, the police discovered that Brevik kept a diary for the previous two years planning the two events. His reason for committing the heinous acts was simply to begin an uprising against the Norwegian government.

It was initially believed that Brevik was insane, but after many evaluations, he was described to have had complete control of his faculties at the time and prior though he did show some tendencies toward narcissism. Though he has been found guilty, he has yet to be sentenced.

# Bonnie and Clyde

Many spree killings are committed by 'lone wolves' or 'partners in crime' type of killers, but so few were committed by what would have normally appeared to be 'America's Sweethearts'. Clyde Champion Barrow and his companion, Bonnie Parker, caused one such horrendous reign of terror. The pair are one of history's most infamous couples, but as with all murderers, they both had their beginnings. To fully appreciate these spree killings, let us look upon the meager beginnings and examine whether or not the source of their discontent can be discovered somewhere along the way.

On a cool day on the first day of October in 1910, a little girl was born to Henry and Emma Parker in Rowena, Texas. They named her Bonnie Elizabeth Parker. Life was fairly normal for little Bonnie until her father died when she was just four years old. Her widowed mother raised her and her siblings alone. Bonnie Parker would not meet until she was working as a waitress at the age of nineteen. She was visiting a friend's house who also turned out to be a friend of the Barrows. However, not many realize this fact, but she was already married. At the age of sixteen, she married a man named Roy Thornton. Thornton was known for being a drunkard and abusive, but Bonnie never filed for divorce. Thornton was arrested very soon after their marriage and placed in a work camp in Texas. It was while her husband was in jail that she met Clyde Barrow and had become instantly smitten with him. She considered him to be her 'true love'.

Clyde Champion Barrow was born March 24, 1909 as the fifth child of seven born to his parents, Henry and Cubie. He, along with two of his siblings, supported themselves through stealing during the times of the Great Depression. The Great Depression was known for creating many criminals—not because those people sought crime, but because they were simply desperately starving and homeless due to the economy.

It was not very long after Bonnie and Clyde met that Clyde was arrested and sent to prison. That incarceration seemed to be a turning point for young Clyde. He entered the prison as a 'gentle, nice boy', but exited as a cold and calculating criminal.  Bonnie hoped to convince Clyde to mend his ways, but as history would have it, he turned her to a life of crime that would eventually end in a hail of bullets.

Their crime spree began with petty theft in 1932 with small robberies at stores and gas stations in an attempt to collect money and weapons so that they could launch a raid on Eastham prison.  They were caught and charged with the crimes, but Barrow only served a few months.  The authorities failed to indict Bonnie due to insufficient evidence.  It was only a matter of a few weeks before Bonnie and Clyde were reunited.  The pair began their twenty-one month long crime spree after this.

Time passed and the rampage continued with each crime causing the death of anyone who interfered with the intention of the couple and their gang.  It was not until 1934 that the end of their reign of terror would surmise.  Clyde, along with some help from Bonnie, organized the escape of several of his gang from Eastham Prison.  Finally, he had gained his revenge on the Texas Department of Corrections by bringing them negative publicity.  During this escape, Major Joe Crowson was shot by Joe Palmer.  Bonnie and Clyde's undoing would be due to the betrayal of Henry Methvin.

After another incident in which two Texas Highway Patrolmen were shot, the court of public opinion turned against Bonnie and Clyde.  In the fallout, a bounty was placed upon their head for the sum of one thousand dollars plus another five hundred added by the governor of Texas.  They wanted them dead, not alive.  However, one turn of event suggests that after killing a sixty year old constable in Commerce, Oklahoma, Barrow, Methvin, and Parker kidnaped the police chief of Commerce and brought him to the state line between Oklahoma and Kansas.  It was there that the trio gave Percy Boyd a change of clothes, some money, and a request from Bonnie to make sure he told the newspapers that she did not smoke cigars.

It was not long after the April kidnapping of Boyd in 1934 that Bonnie Parker and Clyde Barrow met their end.  They were ambushed on May 23rd that year in Bienville Paris, Louisiana.  Six police officers, four of whom were Texas lawmen, assaulted their car in a hailstorm of bullets as they were driving Methvin to see his family in Louisiana.

Despite the anger from many of the victims' families, the couple had achieved a level of fame that was quite congruent with the criminals of that time such as John Dillinger and Al Capone.  Bonnie's mother wanted to bring her daughter home to be buried, which defied Bonnie's wish to be buried next to Clyde, but the crowd of twenty thousand people attending her funeral made that impossible.

It was the crime spree of Bonnie and Clyde, the modern day Romeo and Juliet, which led to kidnapping and bank robberies to become federal offenses, which meant that it now involved the Federal Bureau of Investigation.

# Pretty Boy Floyd

Charles Arthur Floyd was born February 3, 1904 in Georgia. His family moved to the Midwestern United States a few years later. In 1922 at the age of eighteen years, he was arrested for the first time for stealing coins from a post office. In 1925, just three years later, he definitely moved up in the crime world and committed a payroll robbery in September of that year. It was for that crime that he was arrested and later sentenced to five years in prison. He gained parole, however, after only serving just over half of that sentence.

Prison life did not suit Charles very well. Upon his exit from prison, he swore he would never see the inside of another cell again. Rather than making that come true by mending his ways, he made the acquaintance of many already established criminals in Kansas City, Missouri. Over the next several years, he committed a string of bank robberies. It was through his identification by the payroll master and those he robbed that he earned his moniker, "Pretty Boy". He was described as such due to his child-like cheeks.

By the time 1929 rolled around, he became a wanted man for many other cases. That year, he was arrested during an investigation into the string of robberies, vagrancy, highway robbery, but he was always released. That was, he was released until he went to Pueblo, Colorado. There, he was charged with vagrancy, fined, and sentenced to two months in jail.

One of his many aliases was that of 'Frank Mitchell'. It was under this alias that Charles Arthur Floyd was charged with the murder of a police officer who had been shot and killed during a robbery. In Toledo, Ohio, he was arrested and then convicted of the murder of the police officer. Floyd was handed down a sentence of twelve to fifteen years. Yet, Floyd held true to his word that he would not be imprisoned again and he escaped.

After his escape, Floyd went on to be suspected in the murder of Wally and Boll Ash. The Ash brothers were bootleggers who may have been in competition with Floyd and his gang. The pair was found dead as their car burned in March of 1931. It would only be another month before one of the members of Floyd's gang was proven to have killed Officer Castner of Bowling Green, Ohio. Another few months later, Floyd killed an ATF agent in Kansas City, Missouri. The following year, another police officer, Erv Kelly, was murdered as he attempted to arrest Charles Arthur Floyd in April of that year. The following November, Floyd and his gang made an attempt to rob a bank in Boley, Oklahoma.

Though he committed many heinous crimes, he was favored by the general public. He was dubbed as a 'Robin Hood' of his time. This was because during his bank robberies, mortgage documents and other documents that proved a citizen's debt were destroyed in the fray. This freed many people from their mortgages because without proof, the bank could no longer collect on the loan. It was to such a great extent of favor that led to him being protected by the citizens of Oklahoma.

In June of 1933, Floyd and another member of his gang, Adam Richetti, were the primary suspects in the Kansas City Massacre. It was in this event that four of the city's law enforcement officers were killed causing J. Edgar Hoover to dispatch the Federal Bureau of Investigation to go after Floyd. It is possible that one of his other gang members actually participated in the murder spree. Sol Weismann strongly resembled Floyd with his cherub cheeks, and Floyd vehemently denied any involvement because he was attempting to free a friend of his by the name of Frank Nash. In the attempt to free Nash, it was said that Floyd and his friend, Adam Richetti, aided Miller in his foiled attempt to free Nash from police custody. So, this means that had they been present at this event, they could not have been present at the Kansas Massacre.

The death of Charles Arthur "Pretty Boy" Floyd occurred on October 22, 1934 when he was just thirty years old. At the time, he was considered to be Public Enemy Number One following the death of John Dillinger the previous July. His death occurred while law enforcement was in pursuit following another robbery. He hid behind a corn field where he was shot by agents and local law enforcement.

# Dylan Klebold and Eric Harris

Sometimes, those who are innocent carry out the most heinous of acts in our lives. On April 20, 1999, one of the world's most horrible acts committed by children occurred at the Columbine High School in Littleton, Colorado by two high school seniors. The attack was not based upon religion or any other reason beyond the simple act of bullying.

Eric David Harris was born on April 9th, 1981 in Kansas. Due to his father being in the Air Force as a transport pilot, his father was relocated to Littleton, Colorado where he subsequently retired. His mother was a stay at home mom. The family wanted to make a life for themselves in the quiet little town. Neither parent knew what would have transpired as their child grew up and made friends with Dylan Klebold.

Dylan Klebold was a native of Colorado born to parents Thomas and Susan Klebold. The family was devout Lutheran, but did maintain some of his mother's family's Jewish traditions. Because of his intellect, young Dylan always had trouble fitting in.

The pair were instant friends who had something in common— both boys were bullied by other kids for their shy nature and their intelligence. Both Harris and Klebold were active in the drama department, produced videos, and also became computer assistants to help maintain the school's main computer server at Columbine High School. Columbine High School is a small high school with approximately 1700 students attending the facility, which was established in 1973.

Leading up to the event, history looked back on the events that transpired previously. The boys were rumored to have belonged to a group of kids dubbed 'The Trench Coat Mafia', but no official connection was made beyond the rumors. It was also around this time that the pair began tinkering with pipe bombs. However, nothing was suspected because on April 17th, Dylan Klebold even attended the prom with Robyn Anderson, one of his classmates.

Both boys were avid gamers. They would often connect their personal computers on a network and play games such as Doom and

Quake. Oddly enough, Harris used a moniker online that matched the mascot for the school—Reb. Many of the online chatrooms became a forum for Klebold and Harris to spout their hatred for society and certain other people in their neighborhoods. The two were so skilled with computers that they created a video project called *Hitmen for Hire*. In this video, they used a multitude of profane phrases, made statements of violence, and acted out a school shooting. This seemed to be a precursor of things to come. This video was made in December of 1998.

Prior to the events on April 20, 1999, the Jefferson County Sheriff's Office drafted an arrest warrant for a direct threat on a classmate in March of 1998. That warrant, though, was never officially filed. The event that caused this was that Harris made threats against another student by the name of Brooks Brown after the two stopped being friends. That was not the only brush with the law that Klebold or Harris experienced. The pair was known for breaking into a locked van and were caught with stolen computers. Four charges were pressed against the pair, but they were sentenced to a program to help them. Upon completion of that program, their records for those crimes would be expunged. Their sentence was to perform community service, attend psychiatric treatment, and stay out of trouble. Klebold was described as a highly intelligent person who seemed to lack the realization that hard work was required to fulfill his dream.

Just a few short months later on April 20, 1999, Eric Harris and Dylan Klebold made their grand entrance on the campus of Columbine High School. The pair missed that morning's classes, but they were spotted by Brooks Brown as they arrived at lunch time. Brooks states that he was told by Harris to leave campus. As he did, the first shots were fired that left thirteen dead and twenty-four injured. Brown was the one who reported the crime to the authorities.

The shots began in the parking lot and then the boys made their way to the cafeteria. This is where they attempted to detonate two twenty pound bombs, but the devices failed to ignite. The boys began to open fire again once they realized the devices were not going to detonate. After that, they headed toward the library where the majority of their victims were shot and killed.

By that time, Dylan Klebold had already arrived at the school in a separate car and the two boys left two gym bags, each containing a 20-pound propane bomb, inside the school cafeteria. When these devices failed to detonate, Harris and Klebold launched a shooting attack against their classmates. It remains the deadliest attack ever perpetrated at an American high school. Harris was responsible for eight of the 13 confirmed deaths (Rachel Scott, Dan Rohrbough, a teacher identified as Dave Sanders, Steve Curnow, Cassie Bernall, Isaiah Shoels, Kelly Fleming, and Daniel Mauser), while Klebold was responsible for the remaining five (Kyle Velasquez, Matthew Kechter, Lauren Townsend, John Tomlin and Corey DePooter). There were 24 wounded, most in critical condition. Following the spray of bullets in the library, Eric Harris and Dylan Klebold placed their guns to their head—Harris in his mouth and Klebold's weapon pressed against his temple—and pulled the trigger at 12:08 pm.

After the spree killings were complete and the two murderers committed suicide, an entire community and nation fell to its knees. Though this type of incident had occurred prior to and since the Columbine murder spree, it was a new technological age in which media began covering more specific details of the crime and more information was allowed on air. Many people questioned how the two boys could have obtained such weapons that they used. At first, many assumed they obtained the weapons from home, but that was not the case. Robyn Anderson, the young lady with whom Dylan Klebold attended the prom, was eighteen at the time and purchased the shotguns for the two. She did cooperate with law enforcement, so no charges were filed. As it turned out, she had no knowledge that they were going to carry out an attack on the school. It was later determined that as for the TEC-DC9 that Harris was in possession of at the time of the shooting was obtained from a firearms dealer by Mark Manes and Philip Duran who later supplied it to Harris and Klebold. As for the pipe bombs, the boys looked up the information for constructing one of these things on the internet through the Anarchist's Cookbook, or so it was believed that this was the source. At the time, the Anarchist's Cookbook was not the only source of information for constructing pipe bombs. Regardless of where the information was obtained, Harris and Klebold purchased the items to make them at a local hardware store. There were two more bombs placed at the corner of South Wadsworth Boulevard and Ken Caryl Avenue which were detonated using timers, but the ones at the school failed to detonate.

The biggest question many people asked across the nation was 'WHY'. To many on the outside, it seemed as if it were an unprovoked attack by two possible psychopaths. Though there was an obvious level of mental instability, a reason beyond the umbrella of mental disorders was searched for and later found through the journals of Dylan Klebold and Eric Harris. The pair were often bullied, but it may have not been the bullying that was the sole reason. It was later discovered that the pair was fascinated with the Nazi way of life and obsessed with the idea of natural selection. Many psychiatrists attempted to define both Harris and Klebold as a psychopathic sadist and motivated by revenge. Yet, the superiority complex both had, the fact both reviled any type of authority, and had an intense need for control over their situations was suggestive of just this.

When children commit heinous acts against other human beings, society turns to look at their parents. They wonder if the parents were involved in the lives of the children or not. Questions surrounding the composition of the family unit—whether a single parent home or a two parent home—or questions of abuse committed by either parent often surface. Dylan Klebold's mom, Susan Klebold, did not speak out about the crime her son was involved in until 2009 in the Oprah magazine. She described the anguish and horror that she was filled with upon learning that her child was the one terrorizing his fellow students. She said that she even hoped he would die before any other children were injured.

# Charles Whitman

Charles Whitman was born on June 24, 1941 in Lake Worth, Florida.  He grew up with a fascination with guns, but he was also a model student during his school years as well as an Eagle Scout.  Though on the surface, he seemed to have the attributes every young man needed, he grew up in a very abusive home.  As a matter of fact, he left home early to escape his father—who was a violent drunk.  He joined the Marine Corps as a sharpshooter after leaving home.  Once he was discharged, he attended the University of Texas.  While in attendance at the University of Texas, he met his wife, Kathryn Leissner.  The pair married in 1962.

Whitman, though a good student as a child, struggled in his college years.  He returned to duty with the Marines in 1963 but discharged again only a year later.  It was after that second discharge that Whitman returned to the University of Texas, but not much changed for him.  He still struggled academically.  When 1966 rolled around, he began having severe migraines and other mental issues.  A therapist he consulted asked him to return the following week, but Whitman never showed.

That same year, Whitman's mother finally made the decision to leave his father.  Little did she realize that the move was not one that would make life more bearable for her.  The apartment she got was near her son's home.  On July 31, 1966 in the evening, Charles Whitman went over to his mother's apartment and stabbed her.  He also shot her and left a note placed near the body stating that he felt her death was the only way she would be able to escape his father.

Whitman returned home after murdering his mother and waited for his wife to fall asleep.  As his wife slept in the bed she had shared with Whitman for the past four years, he stalked upon her and killed her, too.  In the note that he left beside her, he stated that he had no reason that he could come up with for doing this to his wife.  Some speculate that it could have been his way to spare her from the embarrassment of what he was about to do.

The next day, Whitman loaded the trunk of his car with various weapons and other supplies and made his trek to the University of Texas. Wearing his overalls, he arrived by the tower in the center of the university's quad, climbed to the observation deck, and began shooting at people randomly down below.  In a matter of two hours, several people lost their lives due to his rampage.

# Charles Starkweather

Bonnie and Clyde were not the only murderous pair that graced American history. Charles Ray Starkweather was born on November 24, 1938 in Lincoln, Nebraska. His parents were Guy and Helen Starkweather had seven children of which Charles was the third. Though young Charles grew up in a family that was considered the 'working poor', they always had their basic needs met. All of the children were also very well-behaved. Charles' father was a carpenter, but often suffered from rheumatoid arthritis. His mother, during times when his father's arthritis was too much to bear in order to work, would pick up the slack as a waitress.

Though his family life was a good one, Charles Starkweather had very few positive memories from his time at school, as he was often the subject of bullying. It is possible he had a learning disability, as he was a slow learner. It was proven that he did have eye problems, so that is most likely what affected his lack of drive to apply himself in school. However, Charles Starkweather's favorite subject was gym class. It provided him an outlet for his pent up frustrations over the bullying and as he built the muscle, he was able to bully those who had tormented him growing up. Many of his schoolmates describe him as a very nice guy with the ability to become as mean as a rattlesnake if provoked by the slightest thing.

One of the popular movies of the time was *Rebel without a Cause*. Starkweather became obsessed with the movie and the character James Dean portrayed. He altered his hair and clothing to fit the image created by James Dean. He identified with the background of James Dean's on-screen persona and identified with the trouble he endured due to his circumstances. Charles Starkweather began to hate himself and developed an inferiority complex. When a person has an inferiority complex, he or she believes that they cannot succeed at anything and that their failures are the source of their unending unhappiness.

Yet, despite all of this, Starkweather managed to find something that made him smile. In 1956, he met a girl named Caril Ann Fugate. At the time, he was eighteen and she was thirteen. He quit school to work at a newspaper warehouse near where Caril went to school. His employer commented on his intelligence, or lack thereof, and expressed that he would have to be told multiple times how to do one thing. Charles Starkweather began working as a garbage collector after quitting his job at the warehouse as his existentialist views worsened and he began plotting his life of crime. The garbage route allowed him to plan his bank robberies.

Though he was a thief, Charles Starkweather did not commit his first murder until 1957. It was then that he attempted to purchase some small items using credit. In 1957, credit was not used in the manner it was today. It was not common for a person to have credit or a credit card. At that time, if you did not have the money for it, you simply did without in most cases. However, this was not something Starkweather was able to handle. After being denied, he kept returning for other smaller items until he determined that he was alone with the store attendant. Then, he produced a shotgun, robbed the station attendant, and drove him to a desolate area. It was there that he killed the attendant by shooting him in the head.

The death of the station attendant caused Charles Starkweather to believe that the act itself allowed him to transcend his circumstances and his existence. He grew to believe that he was now above the law. That event was not the beginning of his true spree, but it did break that one barrier he had yet to cross before.

In 1958, his true murder spree began when he attempted to see his girlfriend, Caril Ann Fugate. As he arrived at her home, her parents told him that she was not there. They also told him that he needed to stay away from her and was not welcome in their home any longer. That was the moment in which his switch flipped and he murdered Velda and Marion Bartlett. He also killed Caril Ann's two year old sister by strangulation.

Rather than express horror and shock at the actions of her lover as she arrived home to find her boyfriend killed her family, she helped him hide the bodies behind the house. They soon left and drove to Bennet, Nebraska to a family friend's house. They shot August Meyer and his dog by shooting them in the head with the same shotgun, which he had previously used on Fugate's stepfather and her mother.

After they left Meyer's home, they ended up getting their car stuck in the mud. They left the vehicle behind and walked for a short while until two local teenagers stopped to give them a lift. It was customary in that time to give hitchhikers a ride in that time as people had very little fear of strangers, but the two teens would soon learn the hardest lesson of their lives when Starkweather forced them to drive back to Bennet. He shot the boy, Robert Jensen, and later killed Carol King after a failed rape attempt. Caril Ann was not innocent in this as one would imagine. She attacked the fresh corpse of Carol King in a jealous rage and mutilated her genitalia.

After murdering Jensen and King, Charles and Caril Ann drove the teens' car to the more affluent area of Lincoln, Nebraska. They murdered everyone in the house of C. Lauer Ward, stole their car, and jewelry. The pair even murdered the family dog. This murder caused all of the law enforcement agencies to launch a major manhunt for Fugate and Starkweather. The governor of Nebraska, Victor Anderson, enlisted the aid of the Nebraska National Guard. The National Guard, along with the City of Lincoln police department, searched the entire city block by block. All sightings were reported.

Because they were now high profile criminals, Fugate and Starkweather decided that they needed to ditch the car of the well-to-do Wards. After coming across a man named Merle Collison, who was a traveling salesman sleeping in his Buick in Wyoming, they woke him up and shot him. Afterwards, they attempted to steal his car, but something in the car's design prevented him from being able to drive it very far. The car had something called a 'push-pedal emergency brake'. Starkweather had never used one of these before, so the car ended up stalling. Another motorist saw him struggle and attempted to help, but only to Starkweather's detriment. Starkweather fought with the motorist, but a sheriff happened to pass by and see the fight. That was when Fugate turned in Starkweather to the sheriff, but both were captured—thus ending Starkweather's reign of terror.

Starkweather and Fugate both were extradited to Nebraska after their arrest. It was interesting to discover that the pair turned on each other. Fugate claimed Starkweather kidnapped her, but the judge did not believe it at all. Oddly enough, the only murder Starkweather was tried and convicted for was the murder of Robert Jensen. However, that is all that was needed as he was given the death penalty. He was sentenced to die by electrocution. His sentence was carried out on June 25, 1959 just after midnight. Caril Ann Fugate was sentenced to life, but was later released in 1976 after just over seventeen years of her sentence.

## Harold Shipman

Not all spree killers come from impoverished backgrounds or abusive homes. Sometimes, they are cut from the finest cloth imaginable. One such man was Harold Shipman.

Born on January 14, 1946 to Harold, Sr. and Vera Shipman as the second of four children, he was raised on the Bestwood Council Estate that existed in Nottingham, England. He was raised as a Methodist, and very close to his mother. Unfortunately, his mother passed away when he was only seventeen years old. His mother had lung cancer, which at the time was not treatable other than to make the patient as comfortable as possible. The further that her disease progressed, her physician began to administer morphine. Young Shipman watched his mother's pain abate as she slipped into a peaceful death in June of 1963.

It is speculated that Shipman desired to become a physician because of what he witnessed and his desire to help people. He attended Leeds School of Medicine. Upon graduation in 1970, he immediately began working at the Pontefract General Hospital. In 1974, he transferred to Abraham Ormerod Medical Center as a general practitioner. However, a year later, he was caught abusing the prescription drug pethidine. Pethidine is an opioid pain medication similar to oxycodone—both of which have a highly addictive nature. After he was caught, he was forced to attend a drug rehabilitation clinic. Two years after that incident, he moved to Donneybrook Medical Center near Manchester.

For the next decade, he worked at Donneybrook Medical Center until he started his own surgical center in 1993. The respect for him among the medical community grew which led to him being interviewed about his views on the treatment of the mentally ill. All of that was about to come to an end in 1998. Deborah Massey noticed an anomaly among the corpses that came through her employer's funeral home. She noticed that there was a high rate of death among the patients of Harold Shipman—especially the high number of cremations among his elderly patients. Though the police were involved in the investigation, nothing was found that would bring charges against Shipman.

Shipman's horrors were not over yet, despite the limelight. The one murder that brought his horrors to light was the inquiry launched by Angela Woodruff who was the granddaughter of Kathleen Grundy. Grundy was the latest victim of Shipman. Her death certificate cited 'old age' as the cause of death, but the problem that caused an inquiry to be raised was the fact that her last will and testament bequeathed everything to her physician—Dr. Harold Shipman. An exhumation order came for the body of Kathleen Grundy in which the drug, diamorphine, was discovered in her system. Further investigation established there was a pattern of lethal dosages in other deaths Shipman signed off for as well as the falsification of medical records citing poor health of his patients.

After he was caught, his trial began in October of 1999. He was charged with fifteen deaths of his patients between the years of 1995 and 1998, but it was shown to be a total of two hundred and fifty of his patients suffered death at his hands. Shipman vehemently denied guilt in causing the deaths of the fifteen for which he was sentenced for in addition to the other deaths for which he was not charged.

Once he was found guilty, he was sentenced to serve his time at Wakefield Prison. On January 13, 2004, he was found dead in his cell from asphyxia caused by hanging himself.

## Andrew Cunanan

In 1997, the world lost fashion designer Gianni Versace to the horrible crime of murder. His killer was named Andrew Cunanan. Andrew Cunanan murdered four other people, as well as Versace, during his murder rampage.

Andrew Cunanan was not always a murderer. He was born to Modesto Cunanan and Mary Anne Schillaci in National City, California on August 31, 1969. His father was Filipino American and his mother was Italian American. He was the last child that the couple had. Cunanan grew up with three older siblings. However, his father was deployed to Vietnam on the day Andrew was born.

Young Andrew had a relatively normal upbringing. His parents raised him just like they did the older three. His father even arranged to have him enroll in The Bishop's School in San Diego, California where it was discovered that he was highly intelligent. The school arranged to have his I.Q tested and his score was one hundred and forty seven. The largest problem Cunanan had was that he had a penchant for telling tall tales, especially about his family life and at home. He also was highly skilled at adapting his appearance to look like a completely different person—just like a chameleon.

He graduated from high school in 1987. That fall, he attended University of California in San Diego as an American History major. He discovered that college life was not for him, and he dropped out. After dropping out, he began going to gay bars and became a high-end male prostitute. He also began stealing and dealing in drugs.

In 1988 at the age of nineteen, he left his family and disappeared. His mother, however, found out where he was staying. She also discovered that he was gay. In the 80's, it was not accepted at all to be homosexual and not many families understood. The pair argued and during that argument, Cunanan shoved his mother against the wall so hard that it dislocated her shoulder.

Those years for Cunanan were difficult as he began wrestling with who he truly was. It was suspected in hindsight that he may have suffered from an antisocial personality disorder, but those years were quiet for him. Things changed in April of 1997 when Jeffrey Trail, a United

States Naval Officer, was murdered. Police investigated and all signs pointed to Cunanan.

The next one of Cunanan's friends, an architect by the name of David Madson, turned up dead on the eastern shore of Rush Lake in Minnesota just four days after Jeffrey Trail was murdered. The connection was instantly realized due to the location of the discovery of Trail's body—in the closet of the home of David Madson. The next man to suffer at the hands of Cunanan was Lee Miglin who was a well-known real estate developer. His death occurred just five days after the Madson murder.

Only another five days went by when the fourth victim was discovered in New Jersey. The body was discovered at Finn's Point National Cemetery. The body belonged to the caretaker of the cemetery by the name of William Reese. What was interesting about the case was that after the murder of William Reese, Cunanan was able to hide in full view in Florida.

His fifth and final murder was that of Gianni Versace on July 15, 1997. One of the people who saw Cunanan murder Versace tried to catch him, but failed. He was able to give an accurate description, though. Near the murder scene at a garage where Cunanan stayed, all sorts of documents were found showing Cunanan's aliases.

Eight days later, Cunanan was found with his brains blown out at his own hand inside of a houseboat in Miami. The weapon of choice was a Taurus PT100 pistol, semi-automatic. The weapon was stolen from the first victim and used on the second and third. To this day, no one has ever been able to determine the motives behind the murders.

# Joanna Dennehy

Most people have the concrete belief that the primary prerequisite of being a spree killer, serial killer, or mass murderer of any kind is that one must be a male. That is not always the case and was not with one particular killer by the name of Joanna Dennehy. What made the case the most interesting is that she was the epitome of the textbook serial killer.

In March of 2013 in the United Kingdom, three bodies were found in the ditch in Peterborough. The three males were discovered with stab woulds. Her desire was to kill a total of nine people, but luckily, she was stopped before she attained her goal. During her trial that November, she pleaded guilty to the three murders and an addition two attempted murders. Family members of Dennehy reported that she only plead guilty because of her desire to control the situation. Her method of murder was to stab the men in the heart after luring them with her feminine wiles. Still, the murders were not determined to be sexually motivated.

She soon met a man by the name of Kevin Lee and Paul Creed. Kevin was Joanna's land lord, and Paul was Kevin's business partner. She lured Lee with a story about her father raping her and forcing her to abort her baby, but Creed was still leery.

Her first victim was named Lukasz Slaboszewski. He went to meet up with her in a home. That was when she seduced him and then stabbed him. She killed two other men in two more days—John Chapman and Kevin Lee. Chapman's autopsy report revealed that he was high and drunk at the time of his death. She later described the murders as 'fun'.

Though she was considered an anomaly because she was female, the instances of female serial killers have increased drastically since 1950 as well as the method of murder chosen. Before, they were using more discreet methods. Since the 1950's however, female serial killers have been using knives and guns just as their male counterparts.

What made Joanna Dennehy turn to a life of crime?  No one seems to know.  According to her siblings, she had one of the best childhoods a person could have.  Her life growing up was normal, grades were exceptional, and her parents often doted on her.  However, she ran away from home at the age of fifteen.  Despite her parents many attempts to return their daughter to her home, she turned sixteen—something that now made her untouchable by the law in her home state.

# Adam Lanza

One of the worst and most heart-wrenching spree killings took place at Sandy Hook Elementary School in Sandy Hook, Connecticut. The perpetrator was a former student of the school who, at the time, was twenty years old with no prior criminal record. Adam Peter Lanza was born on April 22, 1992.

He was described by other students in Newtown High School, which he attended for two years, as being intelligent but socially awkward. His parents removed him from school when he turned sixteen years old and homeschooled him. He earned his GED and then attended Western Connecticut State University. Adam Lanza did have the neurological disorder called Autism Spectrum Disorder. According to the Diagnostic Statistical Manual V recently released (after the Sandy Hook shooting), in which Autism Spectrum Disorder includes Asperger's. Lanza was actually diagnosed with Asperger's originally. He also suffered from OCD and sensory integration disorder.

One of the characteristics of Autism Spectrum Disorder is that the individual becomes hyper focused on one particular subject or event. For Lanza, it was mass shootings. The events of Columbine High School and at Northern Illinois University fascinated him. He was also particular about allowing people into his bedroom. Before the shooting, he isolated himself and refused to communicate with anyone other than his mother and only by email with her. He also suffered from a self-induced malnutrition due to his anorexia.

On a cold morning in Newtown, Connecticut, Adam Lanza made his way to the campus of Sandy Hook Elementary school after killing his mother at home and killed twenty children and six adults. When police arrived, that was when Adam Lanza shot himself in the head.

The details of that event are as follows:

- 9:00 am (EST)—Adam shot his mother with a .22 caliber rifle.

- 9:35 am—Adam used the Bushmaster rifle belonging to his mother to blow apart the glass doors to open and began his murder spree
- 9:40 am—Adam shot himself following the twenty six murders.

# Psychology of a Spree Killer

So, what really makes any person kill?  Mass shootings are most often a result of the culprit seeking revenge—thus the reason for the location of the murders (i.e a school or the workplace).  There are often many psychological aspects to the mind of any killer.  Some risk factors such as a history of abuse or neglect, severe interest in arson, hurting animals, or lack of compassion as well as empathy.  Murderers, rather those not committed as an act of passion or revenge, often see their targets as objects rather than actual people.  In addition to that, there are some spree killers who are obsessed with guns or violent games/movies to their own detriment.  Most of the time, spree killers feel powerless and feel that committing the acts of murder are the only way that he or she can regain their power.

Still, nothing or no one can predict that by exhibiting those exact traits whether or not a person will become a murderer.  As a matter of fact, anyone can be considered at risk for becoming a murder if an interest in violent games or movies was a risk factor.  Some people prefer to watch them, but keep it at a distance.

www.ingramcontent.com/pod-product-compliance
Lightning Source LLC
Chambersburg PA
CBHW070940290526
45795CB00003B/1091